Front Cover

1. Shrimp Boat

2. Cranberry Pork Pie

3. Tortilla Stack

Inside Front Cover

1. Tamale Pie

2. French Canadian Toutière

3. Pirozhky

The Humble Pie

The Humble Pie

TERESA KENNEDY

COLLIER BOOKS

Macmillan Publishing Company • New York

Maxwell Macmillan Canada • Toronto

Maxwell Macmillan International
New York • Oxford • Singapore • Sydney

Collier Books
Macmillan Publishing Company
866 Third Avenue
New York, NY 10022

Maxwell Macmillan Canada, Inc.
1200 Eglinton Avenue East
Suite 200
Don Mills, Ontario M3C 3N1

Macmillan Publishing Company is part of the Maxwell Communication Group of Companies.

Library of Congress Cataloging-in-Publication Data
Kennedy, Teresa.
The humble pie / Teresa Kennedy. — 1st Collier Books ed.
p. cm.
Includes index.
ISBN 0-02-034065-6
1. Entrées. 2. Pies. 3. Low-fat diet. 4. Salt-free diet.
I. Title.
TX740.K463 1993   93-1034
641.8'2—dc20   CIP

Macmillan books are available at special discounts for bulk purchases for sales promotions, premiums, fund-raising, or educational use. For details, contact:
Special Sales Director
Macmillan Publishing Company
866 Third Avenue
New York, NY 10022

Cover design by Wendy Bass
Cover photographs by Ellen Silverman
Food styling by Kevin Crafts
Book design by Chris Welch
Illustrations by Larry Berzon

First Collier Books Edition 1993
10 9 8 7 6 5 4 3 2 1
Printed in the United States of America

TO MYLES O'CONNOR
FOR ALL YOU DID.

Contents

My special thanks to Andrew Earley, Linda Nagle, Erin Hart, Carolyn Rainey, Gail Nielsen, Betty Anne Crawford, and Susan Protter for their comments, compliments, criticisms, and ability to eat endless pies.

Introduction

Changing life-styles, changing budgets, and changing eating habits have affected all of us, but most of all the aficionados of good cooking. In recent years, food fans have eaten their way through an astonishing series of culinary fads and fashions, regions, and essential spices. Trendy cuisines seem to come and go with bewildering regularity. To make matters worse, we are continually faced with endless cautions about food—what's good for you and what's bad, until no one, it seems, knows quite what to eat anymore.

Yet some things are indeed abiding, and some of the rules never change. Fresh is best, whole foods are better than processed, and last we heard, there are still four food groups and people need to eat from each of them in order to stay healthy and strong. Finally, and ultimately most important, is that whatever the individual cook's choice or combination of ingredients in cooking, the end result ought to taste good. But if some of the rules never change, some of the problems never do, either. And even the most dedicated of contemporary cooks are faced with the same ones again and again—variety, limited time, limited budgets, good health, and yes, the need for some plain old inspiration to answer that eternal question: What do I make for dinner?

And that is where this book comes in. Every culture and cooking tradition boasts at least one variation on the popular concept of one-dish dining, and this collection reveals a number of fascinating variations on a truly classic theme.

Although the main-dish pie has never become as popular in America as it has throughout the rest of the world, it is my own feeling that it is an idea whose time has very definitely come. As cooks the world over have long known, main-dish pies are easy, economical, and nutritious. They save time and stretch ingredients, yet remain rich in flavor and food value. Far more than the typical American cook's notion of the manufactured, starchy, salty, generally frozen, pot pie, the main-dish pie is truly a staple of international cuisine for peasant and yuppie alike.

My own research into many traditional recipes has yielded some surprisingly contemporary recipes for dishes that are healthy, wholesome, and nourishing. Because the traditional main-dish pie is an invention that arises more from necessity than an excess of ingredients, these are recipes that have much to show the contemporary cook about economy, nutrition, and health. Traditional recipes for the humble pot pie, for example, call for a pastry that uses little or no lard or shortening, but rather is using a combination of flour and broth, with no sacrifice in flavor as a result. Things we now have to be aware of in cooking, like too much fat or salt, were once considered precious ingredients to ordinary cooks and for that reason, they were used sparingly in everyday meals. Vegetables were used to stretch meat, and meat sometimes was not available at all, resulting in the use of other important proteins. Tradition even dictates that pies be round, an inspiration of early cooks who used round pans with sloping sides to literally cut corners and save on ingredients.

Yet, what goes around comes around. Thus, these humble, main-dish pies become the kind of cuisine most modern cooks are looking for—an approach to food that truly combines good sense with good eating.

Finally, and perhaps most importantly, these are the kind of recipes that are, quite simply, fun to cook. It is the kind of cooking that invites new inventions and experimentation. The combination of ingredients and seasonings that can go into a humble main-dish pie are infinite and inspiring. So let these recipes be more your guide than your bible and use them to begin your own culinary adventures. And do remember that despite the need for moderation, the reduction of fats and calories, and simple economy, ultimately cooking should be just that—an adventure.

As someone very wise once said: Cooking is like love—it should be entered into with abandon or not at all.

The Humble Pie

Hints and Pointers

Rolling and Handling Pastry Dough

Even though many people are a little bit leery of pie pastry, there is really nothing to it. The universal rules of thumb are as follows: Don't overhandle or overblend pie pastry; a light hand gets the best result. For biscuit-type crusts, the same holds true—use a light hand during blending, rolling, and baking. Tender pastry depends on small amounts of shortening, butter, or oil forming fine layers or pockets between layers of flour, blended with water or milk. Too much blending destroys these pockets and thus the tender, flaky quality of good pastry and light biscuits.

Oil-based pastries, while desirable for their lower amounts of saturated fats, come with their own set of cautions. They can stand more handling than shortening or butter-based pastries, but they tend in general to be tougher in texture when rolled and placed in baking dishes. Be sure to add enough milk or other liquid with these temperamental types, and don't be shy about mending tears with your fingertips. The baked results won't disappoint you!

To keep bottom crusts crisp during baking, it is not always necessary to prebake the crust. Try putting the prepared crust in the freezer for a few minutes while preparing the filling ingredients. Bake as usual, and you'll be surprised at the results.

Another method for keeping bottom crusts from getting soggy during baking is to sprinkle them with a thin layer of instant mashed potato flakes.

By and large, pies with a bottom crust always bake better on the bottom rack of the oven. However, bake deep-dish or casserole-type pies with a top crust on the center rack of the oven for best results.

To prevent double-crust pies from leaking while they bake, you must make sure that the top crust is folded over the bottom crust before crimping the edge, and that the crust is adequately pierced to allow steam to escape during baking. Also be sure not to trim the edge too closely. A high crimped edge will contain filling better than a close-trimmed one.

Some Substitutions

Everyone seems to be increasingly concerned about lower fat and cholesterol cooking these days, and while the recipes contained in the pages of this book have been composed with an eye to more modern tastes and diets, some further substitutions for even lighter and/or restricted diets are as follows:

Eggs: For reduced cholesterol, try the simplest alternative—use medium-size eggs, rather than extra large or jumbo. It may not be a big reduction in your cholesterol count, but it does help!

For those on cholesterol-restricted diets, two egg whites can be substituted in many recipes for one whole egg, or try one of the egg substitutes currently available in many supermarkets.

Salt: I've tried a number of the commercial salt substitutes and even light or reduced-sodium salts, and find them either very harsh-tasting or too pallid to bother with. I do, however, highly recommend seasoning blends—lemon pepper, vegetable seasonings, etc.—as a salt substitute. They add so much flavor-wise, you really don't miss the salt!

Butter: I maintain that all the truly sensual people in the world love butter. Confidentially, I've never really found an acceptable substitute. Nonetheless, buttermilk-flavored margarine blends can be good, and cholesterol-free. Also try a combination of butter-flavored granules and an oil low in saturated fat in cooking. A rule of thumb: 1/2 teaspoon butter-flavored granules and 1 tablespoon oil equals 1 tablespoon of butter. Where sautéing in butter or oil is called for in a recipe, try steaming onions, garlic, or the like in 4 tablespoons of water until tender.

Cheese: Look for low-fat and low-sodium cheeses in your supermarket or grocery. They are increasingly available to consumers, and increasingly fine in quality and flavor.

Milk and Cream: Unless otherwise specified, most of the recipes in this book can utilize low-fat or skim milk where milk is called for. Cream is a bit trickier and takes some experimentation. My own discovery in this area is that evaporated milk can usually be substituted for heavy cream and evaporated low-fat milk or even evaporated skim milk for light cream or regular milk. A great way of reducing fat without reducing flavor or that creamy quality.

Crusts

~ Old-time Pie Paste ~

A SURPRISING number of old cookbooks contain recipes for main-dish pies that invariably begin, "First you make a paste . . ." Paste, as described in these wonderful old volumes, and modern pie pastry, I soon discovered, are two different things. Paste for the old-time meat and pot-type pies is less rich in fat and more sturdy than conventional pie pastry as it is meant to seal in juices and flavor during baking. In offering this version for more modern palates, I have found it necessary to compromise only a bit by utilizing a small amount of shortening and further tenderizing the flour, normally the function of larger quantities of fat, by adding a tablespoon of vinegar.

Makes one double-crust or two single-crust pies

2 cups all-purpose or whole-wheat flour
1 teaspoon salt
3 tablespoons all-vegetable shortening
1/2 cup broth (chicken, beef, vegetable, or fish according to pie recipe)
1 tablespoon white vinegar

Combine the flour and salt. Cut in the shortening and blend with your fingertips until the mixture resembles fine crumbs. Add the broth and vinegar and blend until the mixture forms a ball. Alternatively, you may combine all the ingredients in the bowl of a food processor fitted with the metal blade. Using the pulse switch, combine only until the dough holds its shape. Turn out onto a floured surface and roll out to a thickness of about 1/4 inch for bottom crusts and 1/8 inch for top crusts.

⇜ Cornmeal Crust ⇝

CRUNCHY and very slightly sweet, this crust is a marvelous, relative-ly low-fat complement for Empanadas (pages 39-41) or Toutière (page 69). This recipe makes a fair amount of dough. It may be halved suc-cessfully, or one half may be used and the other frozen for later use.
Makes one double-crust pie or twelve individual pies

2 1/2 cups all-purpose flour
1 1/2 cups white or yellow cornmeal
3 tablespoons sugar
1 teaspoon salt
2 tablespoons baking powder
3 ounces cream cheese, softened
3/4 cup (1 1/2 sticks) butter
2 large eggs

In a large bowl, sift together the dry ingredients. Cut in the cream cheese and butter until the mixture is the consistency of coarse crumbs. Add the eggs, one at a time, and mix until the dough comes together to form a ball. The dough will be slightly sticky and somewhat softer than pastry. If the dough seems dry, add 2 or 3 tablespoons of water. Chill 1 hour.

For empanadas, divide the dough into 12 equal portions. On a lightly floured surface, roll each portion out into a 5-inch round and proceed ac-cording to the recipe directions. For a double-crust pie, divide the dough into 2 portions. On a lightly floured surface roll out one portion into a 12-inch circle for a 1-inch-deep pie plate. Fill according to the recipe direc-tions. Roll the remaining portion into a 12-inch round for the top crust. Crimp and trim the edges accordingly.

~Olive Oil Crust~

OLIVE OIL is an incredibly tasty and healthy alternative to solid shortening in pastry. Try this marvelous crust with the Tomato, Cheese, and Basil Tart on page 91. Do note that this dough, as with any oil pastry, is best handled by rolling it out between two sheets of waxed paper or plastic wrap, rather than on a floured surface.

Makes one single-crust pie

1 1/2 cups unsifted all-purpose flour
1/2 teaspoon salt
7 tablespoons extra virgin olive oil (not light or extra light)
3 tablespoons milk

In a medium-size mixing bowl, sift together the flour and salt. Add the olive oil and milk to the flour mixture all at once and stir with a fork until the mixture forms a ball. Flatten slightly. Roll out to the desired shape between sheets of waxed paper or plastic wrap and proceed according to the recipe directions.

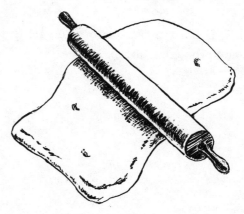

Crusts

~✣Whole-wheat Crust ✣~

Highly recommended for its nutty flavor, crunchy texture, and the health benefits of whole-grain flour. Try this with any of the heartier meat pies.

Makes one double-crust or two single-crust pies

2 cups unbleached all-purpose flour
1 cup whole-wheat flour
1 1/2 teaspoons salt
3/4 cup all-vegetable shortening
8 tablespoons ice water

In a large bowl, sift together the flours and salt. Cut in the shortening until the mixture is the texture of coarse crumbs. Sprinkle the water over the crumb mixture, 1 tablespoon at a time, mixing until the dough forms a ball. Divide the dough into 2 equal portions. On a lightly floured surface, roll out into rounds approximately 1/8 inch thick. Proceed with filling and baking according to the recipe directions.

Variation: For rye crust, substitute 1 cup rye flour for the whole-wheat flour and proceed as above.

Basic Pie Crust

A<small>N EASY TO</small> make and easy to use recipe for basic pie pastry that can be used for all kinds of pies. For pastry novices, there are two important things to remember about making pie crust: Blend the flour and shortening with the fingertips—it's by far the easiest and fastest way to get the "feel" of good pastry—and don't overhandle the dough.

Makes one double-crust or two single-crust pies

2 1/4 cups all-purpose flour
1 teaspoon salt
2/3 cup shortening
4 1/2 tablespoons ice water

In a large mixing bowl, sift together the flour and salt. Cut in the shortening. With your fingertips, combine the flour and shortening until the mixture is the consistency of coarse crumbs. Add the ice water, 1 tablespoon at a time, until the mixture comes together to form a ball. Divide the dough into 2 equal portions. On a lightly floured surface, roll out into rounds to a thickness of approximately 1/8 inch. Transfer to a pie plate or plates, fill, and bake according to the recipe directions.

Popover Crust

CLOSE IN spirit to a Yorkshire pudding, this crust is a light and low-fat alternative to both conventional pastry crusts and puff pastry. Be sure to pour the batter over a hot filling for maximum puff.

Makes one 9 x 13-inch top crust

2 large eggs
1 cup milk
1 tablespoon oil
1 cup all-purpose flour
1/2 teaspoon salt
Grated Parmesan cheese (optional)

Preheat the oven to 400°F. Fill a 9 x 13-inch baking dish with the filling recipe of your choice and heat for 20 minutes, or according to the recipe directions.

Meanwhile, with all the ingredients at room temperature, beat together the eggs, milk, and oil in a large bowl. Add the flour and salt and beat until smooth. Remove the preheated pan from the oven. Pour the batter over the filling, being sure to cover it completely. Sprinkle with Parmesan cheese, if desired. Return the pan to the oven and continue baking until the crust is puffed and golden, approximately 20 minutes.

Polenta

OFTEN SERVED on its own or garnished as an Italian side dish, cornmeal polenta makes the perfect complementary crust to any number of recipes. This microwave version is fast and easy, excellent for use with Tex-Mex Polenta Pie (page 48) or experiment!
Makes one 10-inch crust

Two 13 1/2-ounce cans chicken broth or 4 1/2 cups homemade
1 cup yellow cornmeal
3 tablespoons melted butter or olive oil

Whisk together the broth and cornmeal in a large, microwave-safe bowl. Microwave on the high setting until thickened, approximately 15 minutes, whisking every 5 minutes to remove any lumps that may form. Remove the polenta from the microwave and allow it to cool slightly. Stir in the butter or olive oil. Turn it into a 10-inch pie plate and pat evenly into a crust. Fill as desired.

Variation: To prepare polenta on top of the stove, bring the broth to the boiling point over medium heat, add the cornmeal all at once, and cook, stirring constantly, until very thick. Proceed as above.

Fougère

SIMILAR TO pâte à choux, that delicate pastry which surrounds cream puffs and eclairs, this crust is excellent with chicken and seafood pies of all kinds.

Makes one 10-inch crust

1/4 cup butter or margarine
3/4 cup cold water
3/4 cup all-purpose flour
1/2 teaspoon salt
3 large eggs

In a medium-size saucepan, bring the butter and water to a boil over high heat. Add the flour and salt all at once. Beat with a wooden spoon until the mixture forms a ball, about 2 minutes. Remove from the heat and add the eggs, one at a time, beating well after each addition. Turn the dough into a lightly greased 10-inch pie plate or baking dish. Fill as desired and bake according to the recipe directions.

Buttermilk Biscuit Crust

T HE SECRET to light and fluffy biscuits is the same as it is for flaky pie pastry—don't overhandle the dough. Overmixing or too much kneading serves to toughen the dough by developing an excess of gluten in the flour. Use this as a topper for all kinds of main-dish pies.

Makes approximately twelve biscuits or one top crust for a 9 x 13-inch pie

2 cups all-purpose flour
2 tablespoons baking powder
2 teaspoons baking soda
4 1/2 tablespoons butter, margarine, or shortening
3/4 cup low-fat buttermilk

In a large mixing bowl, sift together the dry ingredients. With your fingertips or a pastry blender, cut in the butter, margarine, or shortening until the mixture is the consistency of coarse crumbs. Add the buttermilk all at once and blend to make a stiff dough. Turn the dough out onto a lightly floured surface and knead lightly. Drop it by tablespoonfuls onto the filling or, if desired, pat the dough out to a 1/2-inch thickness and cut into rounds with biscuit cutter. Arrange the biscuits on top of the prepared filling and bake according to the recipe directions.

Sourdough Pie Crust

SOURDOUGH starter is easy to make and wonderful to have on hand, not only for those marvelous sourdough breads, but also for some lesser-known alternatives, such as pancakes and this fabulous pie crust. This recipe may be halved for a single-crust pie, or if preferred, one crust may be frozen for another use.

SOURDOUGH STARTER
Makes just over 2 cups

1 1/4 teaspoons (1/2 envelope) dry yeast
2 cups all-purpose flour
2 tablespoons sugar
2 1/2 cups water

In a medium-size bowl, beat all the ingredients together until smooth. Cover the mixture loosely with a lid or cloth and allow it to stand in a warm place for 2 or 3 days. The starter is ready to use when it is bubbling and lively. Store starter in the refrigerator.

SOURDOUGH PIE PASTRY

Makes one double-crust or two single-crust pies

2 1/2 cups all-purpose flour
1 teaspoon baking soda
1 teaspoon salt
4 tablespoons shortening
1 cup sourdough starter
8 tablespoons cold water

In a large bowl, knead together the flour, soda, salt, and shortening until blended. Add the starter and water and continue kneading until smooth. Form the dough into a ball, cover, and allow to rise 30 minutes. Divide the dough into two equal portions. On a lightly floured surface, roll out one portion to a 10-inch circle. Lift into a 9-inch pie plate, trim the edges, and fill according to the recipe directions. Roll out the remaining dough for the top crust and fit it over the filling. Seal the edges, trim, and bake according to the recipe directions.

Puff Pastry

I HAVE A confession to make—I rarely have the time, to say nothing of the energy, to make my own puff pastry. I've found that using the prepackaged frozen varieties means no real sacrifice in quality and they can be a godsend when you want a fast and elegant housing for almost any main-dish pie filling. Nonetheless, for those purists among you, I include the following, a somewhat abbreviated, but thoroughly delectable version of the classic.

Makes approximately 1 pound

6 1/2 cups unbleached all-purpose flour
1 teaspoon salt
1 pound (4 sticks) unsalted butter, chilled
3/4 to 1 cup ice water

Reserve 3/4 cup of the flour and set aside for flouring the surface used for rolling and kneading. In a large bowl, stir together the flour and salt. Cut 1 stick (1/4 pound) of the butter into tablespoon-size chunks. With your fingertips, incorporate the butter into the flour mixture until it forms coarse crumbs. Sprinkle 3/4 cup water over the flour mixture and blend until it forms a soft dough. Add more water, 1 tablespoon at a time, if the dough seems too stiff. Be careful not to overwork or knead the dough or it will be tough. Form the dough into a ball and flatten slightly. Wrap it in plastic wrap, and chill in the refrigerator for 20 minutes.

While the dough chills, form the remaining chilled butter into a flat square on a lightly floured surface and set aside. Remove the dough from the refrigerator, unwrap it, and roll it out into a circle, about 1/4 inch thick. Place the butter square in the middle of the dough circle and fold edges of the dough up and around the butter to encase it completely. Seal the edges with your fingertips. Roll the dough into a rectangle and chill for 30 minutes.

Roll out the cold dough to a thickness of about 3/8 inch. Fold it in thirds, as if it were a letter. Turn the dough toward you one quarter of a turn, so that the folded edge is to your right. This completes one turn of the dough. Roll it out again and fold it in thirds. Wrap and chill the dough for another 30 minutes.

Repeat the rolling, folding, and chilling for a total of four turns. Proceed according to the recipe directions or store until needed. This dough will keep for up to four months in the freezer or up to a week in the refrigerator.

Cheddar Cheese
❧ Crust ☙

MARVELOUS and easy, this no-roll crust is great with any of the vegetarian pies in this book. Try it for a tasty and nourishing twist.
Makes one single 10-inch crust

1 cup grated cheddar cheese
3/4 cup all-purpose flour
1/2 teaspoon salt
1 teaspoon dry mustard or 1 tablespoon coarse-grained Dijon mustard
1/4 cup melted butter or olive oil

In a medium-size bowl, mix the cheese with the remaining ingredients until well blended and the mixture holds together when pinched with the fingertips. Press the dough evenly over the bottom and sides of a 10-inch pie plate, fill, and proceed according to the recipe directions.

❧ Confetti Crust ❧

FANTASTIC for seafood, cheese, or ground beef-based pies. One of the fastest and easiest crusts around.

Makes one single 9-inch crust

2 cups finely crushed unsalted tortilla or corn chips
2 tablespoons butter or margarine, softened
1/2 teaspoon salt (optional)
2 1/2 teaspoons chili powder

Combine all the ingredients and press into bottom and sides of a 9-inch pie plate. Bake at 375°F for 10 minutes. Cool and fill according to the recipe directions.

～❧ No-roll Pie Pastry ❧～

FAST AND easy, this pie crust is best made in a food processor. Though the use of butter or margarine and egg yolk makes it higher in fat and cholesterol than most of the pastries included here, make no substitutions or the pastry will be tough.

Makes one single 10-inch crust

1/2 cup (1 stick) butter or margarine, cut into chunks
1 1/2 cups all-purpose flour
1 teaspoon salt
1 large egg yolk
2 tablespoons milk

Place all the ingredients in the workbowl of a food processor fitted with the metal blade. Using the pulse switch, process just until the dough is well blended and begins to form a ball. Remove from the bowl and press onto bottom and sides of a 10-inch pie plate. Proceed according to the recipe directions.

Cream Cheese
~ Pastry ~

CREAM CHEESE, lower in fat per portion than either butter or margarine, forms the basis for this dough. An excellent choice for Kulebiaka (pages 83-85) or Pirozhky (pages 80-82).

Makes one double 9-inch crust, one kulebiaka, or twelve pirozhky

1 1/2 cups all-purpose flour
2 teaspoons baking powder
1 large egg
6 ounces cream cheese, softened
4 tablespoons (1/2 stick) butter, cut into small chunks

In a medium-size bowl, sift together the flour and baking powder and set aside. Beat together the egg, cream cheese, and butter. (Note: This doesn't have to be completely blended.) Turn the cream cheese mixture into the flour mixture. With the fingertips, combine until the mixture forms a soft dough. Roll out as desired and proceed according to the recipe directions.

~ *Yogurt Pastry* ~

T HIS IS ONE of the finest pastries on record for those watching their fat intake and is particularly good for Samosas (pages 78-79), Pirozhky (pages 80-82), or any of the richer meat fillings.

Makes one double-crust, two single-crust, or approximately sixteen individual pies

2 cups all-purpose flour
3/4 teaspoon salt
4 tablespoons shortening
3/4 cup plain yogurt

In a large bowl, sift together the flour and salt. With the fingertips, blend in the shortening until the mixture has the consistency of fine crumbs. Add the yogurt and blend until the mixture forms a soft dough. Chill thoroughly and roll out as desired.

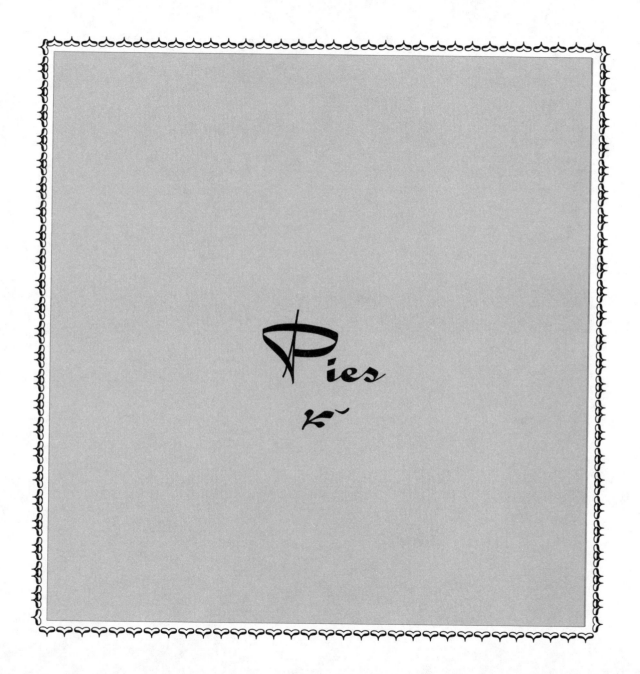

Pies

Jamaican Beef Pie

ALTHOUGH this is usually made as individual turnover-style pies, I like this easy, single-pie version. Serve with a fresh tomato relish, additional hot sauce, and fried plantains.

Serves 6

1 recipe Basic Pie Crust (page 13)
1 pound lean ground beef or 2 1/2 cups roast beef, chopped
3 large cloves garlic, minced
4 scallions, including green tops, chopped
1/2 cup finely chopped green bell pepper
1 medium-size tomato, chopped
2 tablespoons chopped fresh parsley
3 tablespoons Jamaican-style (mild and yellow) curry powder or to taste
2 tablespoons Tabasco or other hot pepper sauce or to taste
1 teaspoon salt
1/4 cup dark rum

Preheat the oven to 400°F.

In a medium-size skillet, sauté the beef, garlic, scallions, and bell pepper over medium heat until the beef loses its pink color. Add the tomato, parsley, curry powder, Tabasco, and salt. Continue cooking, stirring occasionally, for 3 minutes. Add the rum and cook until most of the liquid has evaporated.

Turn the meat mixture into the prepared crust, place the top crust over it, crimp the edges to seal, and trim as necessary. Prick the top crust three or four times with the tines of a fork to allow steam to escape.

Bake for 30 to 35 minutes, or until the crust is lightly browned.

~ Beef and Oyster Pie ~

A N E L E G A N T entree or a party buffet dish, this recipe, in any of its variations, can hardly rate as "humble." Nonetheless, it is well worth the extra effort and expense, and is sure to please.

Serves 6 to 8

1 recipe Whole-wheat Crust (page 12) or 1 recipe Sourdough Pie Crust
*   (pages 18-19) or 1 recipe Puff Pastry (pages 20-21)*
1 1/2 pounds beef rump, sliced very thin and cut into 3-inch strips
2 cloves garlic, minced
Flour seasoned with salt and pepper for dredging
1 1/2 dozen fresh oysters, liquor reserved
3 tablespoons capers, drained
1 large egg, beaten (optional)

Preheat the oven to 425°F. Divide the pastry into 2 equal portions. On a lightly floured surface, roll out half the dough to a thickness of approximately 1/8 inch, and line a deep 9-inch pie plate with it. Roll out the remaining dough into a 12-inch circle and set aside.

Sprinkle the beef with the minced garlic, making sure that the garlic is well distributed among the slices. Allow the beef to come to room temperature.

Dredge the beef slices in the seasoned flour. Cut the oysters in half and roll a half oyster up in a slice of beef. Arrange the rolls in the crust. (They will be piled fairly high.) Sprinkle with the capers. Pour the oyster liquor over all and add enough water so that the liquid comes approximately two thirds of the way up the sides of the dish.

Carefully place the top pastry over all. Crimp the edge by folding the top crust over the bottom crust and sealing the edge with your fingertips.

Do not cut any slits in the crust. Glaze the crust with beaten egg, if desired.

Bake in the preheated oven for 10 minutes, then reduce the oven temperature to 350°F and continue baking for 50 minutes longer, or until the crust is golden brown.

Variations:

Beef and Smoked Oyster Pie: For a richer variation of this recipe, substitute 2 three-ounce cans smoked oysters, drained, for the fresh oysters and half white wine and half water for the liquid, enough so that it comes two thirds of the way up the sides of the dish, approximately 3/4 cup. Proceed as above.

Beef Wellington Pie: Substitute 4 ounces pâté de foie gras for the oysters. Combine with 2 ounces chopped fresh cultivated white mushrooms. Roll approximately 2 teaspoons of this mixture in each slice of beef, and use half red wine and half water for the liquid as above. Proceed as above.

Pies

~❧ Tamale Pie ❧~

A HEARTY AND colorful Southwestern specialty, this is great with a cold Mexican beer.

Serves 6 to 8

1/4 cup milk
3/4 cup yellow cornmeal
1 pound ground beef
1 medium-size onion, chopped
2 cloves garlic, minced
1 large green bell pepper, seeded and chopped
One 8-ounce can tomato sauce
1/2 teaspoon salt
2 tablespoons sugar
3 to 4 tablespoons chili powder or to taste
1 1/2 cups (12 ounces) canned or frozen corn
1/2 cup green olives, with their brine, pitted and chopped
1/4 cup pimentos, drained
1 cup hot water
1 cup grated cheddar cheese

Preheat the oven to 350°F.

In a medium-size bowl, mix the milk and cornmeal and set aside.

Sauté the beef, onion, garlic, and pepper together over high heat in a large sauté pan until the meat is browned. Drain any fat. Add the tomato sauce, salt, sugar, and chili powder. Taste and adjust the seasoning if necessary. Add the corn, olives, and pimentos. Simmer over medium heat, stirring occasionally, for 12 minutes. Remove from the heat and add the cornmeal mixture and hot water.

Pour the mixture into a lightly oiled 9 x 13-inch baking dish or casserole. Bake, covered, for 1 hour. Remove the cover and sprinkle with the grated cheese. Bake, uncovered, for an additional 30 minutes, or until the cheese is bubbly and lightly browned.

Variation: For a vegetarian version of Tamale Pie, substitute one 16-ounce can undrained pink or kidney beans for the ground beef. Reduce the browning time accordingly.

~ Shepherd's Pie ~

SHEPHERD'S pie was originally made with lamb, hence the name. The following recipe uses either lamb or beef and is a wonderful way to use up leftover meat, gravy, and mashed potatoes. If you're like me, however, and rarely have the right amounts of all three on hand, instant mashed potatoes and prepackaged or canned soups or gravies can come in handy.
Serves 6 to 8

1 1/2 cups chopped celery (approximately 4 stalks)
1 large onion, chopped
2 cloves garlic, minced
1/2 cup water
4 cups cubed cooked beef or lamb
2 cups leftover gravy
1/2 cup chopped fresh parsley
1/2 teaspoon crumbled dried rosemary
1 teaspoon salt
2 tablespoons Worcestershire sauce
2 tablespoons ketchup
3 large eggs, separated
3 cups mashed potatoes
Paprika

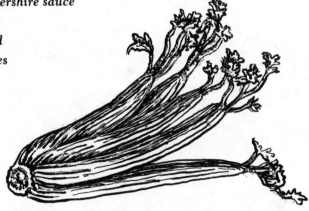

Preheat the oven to 400°F.

In a medium-size skillet or saucepan simmer the celery, onion, and garlic in the water until tender. Combine with the meat and gravy. Stir in the parsley, rosemary, salt, Worcestershire sauce, and ketchup. Turn the mixture into a 2 1/2-quart casserole. Place the casserole in the oven to warm while preparing the potato topping. Beat the egg yolks well and combine with the mashed potatoes. In a separate bowl, beat the egg whites until they form stiff peaks and fold into the mashed potatoes.

Spread the mashed potato topping over the warmed meat mixture. Sprinkle with paprika. Return the pan to the oven and continue baking an additional 25 minutes, or until slightly puffed and lightly browned.

Irish Corned Beef and Cabbage Pie

DESPITE the somewhat misleading name of this recipe, it's great for those wishing to cut their meat intake as there are only 8 ounces of corned beef divided among six portions, slightly over an ounce per person! The small portion of meat enables the thrifty cook to splurge on the finest deli-style corned beef available. I've tried several types of corned beef with this recipe, including homemade and even canned, but deli-style seems to yield the best result. For those inclined to venture into kosher-Gaelic, try pastrami. That's good, too.

Serves 6

1/2 recipe Old-time Pie Paste (page 9) or 1/2 recipe Puff Pastry (pages 20-21) or top the pie with your choice of crumbled, flavored rice cakes

5 cups shredded cabbage

3 tablespoons unsalted butter or extra virgin olive oil

2 tablespoons all-purpose flour

1 cup milk or evaporated skim milk

1 cup grated Gruyère cheese

1/2 teaspoon nutmeg

Dash cayenne pepper

1/2 teaspoon dried dill or 1 tablespoon chopped fresh dillweed

2 tablespoons Dijon mustard

8 ounces good-quality corned beef, cut into 1/4-inch strips

1 large egg, beaten (optional)

Preheat the oven to 400°F.

Cook the cabbage in boiling water for 5 to 8 minutes, or until tender. Drain and set aside.

Heat the butter in a medium-size saucepan over medium heat. Add the flour all at once and blend to make a roux. Cook 2 to 3 minutes, stirring constantly. Add the milk, whisking constantly, until the mixture is smooth and thick, approximately 4 minutes. Add the cheese, blending until melted. Add the seasonings, taste, and adjust if necessary. Combine with the strips of beef and cabbage and turn into a lightly oiled 9 x 13-inch pan.

Top with a layer of pie paste, making sure the edges are sealed over the edges of the pan. If you are using the rice-cake crust, be sure to slide a sheet of aluminum foil under the pan to catch any filling that may boil over during baking. Brush with a beaten egg to glaze the crust, if desired. (The pie may be made ahead and refrigerated at this point, if desired.)

Bake until the pastry is puffed and golden, 45 to 50 minutes. For the rice-cake crust, lessen baking time by 15 minutes. Cut into squares to serve.

~ Cornish Pasties ~

A MIDWESTERN specialty, these hefty pies were used to fill the lunch boxes of Cornish miners. For those who don't have such physical occupations, I suggest—good as they are—that you confine yourself to one. Believe me, you'll know you've eaten!

Serves 6 to 8

1 recipe Whole-wheat Crust (page 12), Old-time Pie Paste (page 9), or
*   Basic Pie Crust (page 13)*
1 1/2 pounds lean round of beef, cut into 1/2-inch chunks
3 potatoes, cut into 1/2-inch cubes
2 carrots, grated (about 1/2 cup)
1/2 cup chopped rutabaga
1 medium-size onion, finely chopped
1 teaspoon salt
Freshly ground pepper to taste
1 tablespoon butter, softened

Preheat the oven to 325°F.

Divide the dough into 6 or 8 equal portions. Roll each portion out into an 8-inch circle.

In a large bowl, combine the meat, potatoes, carrots, rutabaga, and onion. Add the salt, pepper, and butter and mix well.

Place approximately 3/4 cup filling on one half of each circle of dough. Fold the remaining half over the filling, turnover-style, and crimp the edges firmly to seal. Slash each pasty three or four times to allow steam to escape during baking. With a spatula, transfer the pasties to a lightly oiled baking sheet. Bake 1 to 1 1/4 hours, or until lightly browned.

The Humble Pie

⇥ Empanadas ⇤

A SOUTH American specialty, these hand-held, turnover-style pies are spicy and satisfying—perfect picnic fare. While I prefer the cornmeal crust suggested below for its added crunchiness and texture, empanadas can be made with any of the more basic crusts, or if you're in a rush, many grocery stores and supermarkets in major cities now sell prepackaged frozen dough rounds for these wonderful little pies.

One other note: Skin can be sensitive to fiery jalapeño peppers. Try wearing rubber gloves when seeding and chopping the peppers. It works!
Each filling recipe makes twelve empanadas

1 recipe Cornmeal Crust (page 10) or other two-crust pastry recipe

BEEF FILLING
1 large onion, chopped
3 cloves garlic, minced
3 pickled jalapeño peppers, seeded and minced
3 teaspoons ground cumin
1 1/2 tablespoons chili powder
1 teaspoon oregano
1/2 teaspoon ground cloves
2 tablespoons vegetable oil
1 pound ground chuck
One 28-ounce can plum tomatoes in tomato puree, chopped
1/3 cup raisins
3/4 cup pimento-stuffed green olives, sliced
Generous dash Tabasco or other hot pepper sauce or to taste

In a large skillet, sauté the onion, garlic, peppers, and spices in the oil over high heat until the onion is translucent. Add the beef, stirring to break up any lumps, and continue cooking until browned. Add the chopped tomatoes and their puree, raisins, and olives and simmer, stirring frequently, until the liquid has all but evaporated, about 15 minutes. Cool and season to taste with the Tabasco. To assemble, see below.

CHICKEN FILLING
For a kinder, gentler empanada . . .

2 cups cooked chicken, diced
3 tablespoons oil
1 bunch scallions, including green tops, chopped
1/2 cup chopped green bell pepper
1/2 cup pitted black olives, sliced
2 medium-size fresh tomatoes, chopped
One 8-ounce can tomato sauce
1/2 teaspoon salt
1 teaspoon oregano
1 1/2 teaspoons ground cumin
3 tablespoons chili powder
1/2 cup fresh corn (1 cob) or one 8-ounce can corn, drained

In a large skillet, lightly sauté the chicken in the oil over high heat. Add the scallions, green pepper, olives, and tomatoes. Fry gently until the green pepper is tender. Add the tomato sauce, spices, and corn. Cook over medium heat, stirring frequently, until the mixture has thickened and the liquid has all but evaporated. Cool.

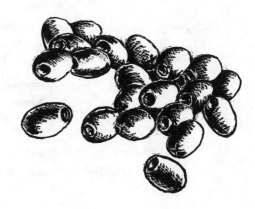

To Assemble the Empanadas

Preheat the oven to 425°F.

Divide the dough into 12 equal portions. On a lightly floured surface, roll out each portion of dough into a 6-inch circle approximately 1/8 inch thick. Place a generous 1/4 cup filling on one half of each circle, to within 1/2 inch of the edge. Fold the dough over the filling to enclose it and seal the edge firmly, wetting your fingertips, if necessary. With a spatula, transfer the empanadas to a nonstick baking sheet. Bake for 20 minutes, or until they are golden brown.

Arkansas Biscuit Chicken Pot Pie

THE USE of evaporated low-fat milk in this recipe rather than the more traditional cream sacrifices nothing in flavor or savory satisfaction.

Serves 6 to 8

1 recipe Buttermilk Biscuit Crust (page 17)
1 to 1 1/2 pounds chicken pieces, uncooked
2 cups water
1 large onion, chopped
2 carrots, scrubbed and diced
3 stalks celery, including leaves, washed and diced
1 cup fresh or frozen peas
1 teaspoon salt
1 tablespoon poultry seasoning or to taste
3 tablespoons all-purpose flour
One 12-ounce can (1 2/3 cups) evaporated low-fat milk
2 tablespoons butter or margarine (optional)

Preheat the oven to 425°F.

In a large saucepan, place the chicken pieces in water and simmer until tender, approximately 15 minutes. Remove them from the water, leaving the water in the pan, and cool.

Place the onion, carrots, celery, and peas in the same water and continue simmering until the broth is reduced by one half and the vegetables are tender. Season to taste with salt and poultry seasoning. Combine the flour with the milk, then whisk it into the broth and vegetables and simmer until thickened and smooth. Remove from the heat.

Skin and bone the chicken pieces, dice the meat and add it to the vegetable mixture. Turn the mixture into a lightly oiled 9 x 13-inch baking dish. Drop the biscuit mixture by tablespoonfuls over the top. Dot with butter, if desired. Bake for 25 minutes, or until the filling is bubbly and the biscuits are golden brown.

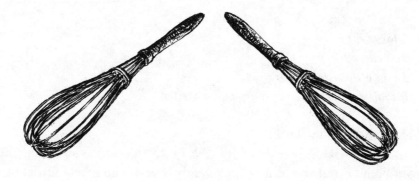

~❧ Turkey Pudding Pie ❧~

IN A VARIATION on an old recipe, turkey, vermouth, and mushrooms are baked in a Yorkshire pudding for a dramatic result.
Serves 6

4 cups diced, cooked turkey
2 teaspoons poultry seasoning
1 cup sliced fresh white cultivated mushrooms
1 medium-size onion, thinly sliced
1/4 cup sweet vermouth
1 recipe Popover Crust (page 14) or use:
   3 large eggs
   1/2 cup milk
   1 cup all-purpose flour
   3 tablespoons butter or margarine, melted

Preheat the oven to 400°F.

In a large sauté pan, combine the turkey, poultry seasoning, mushrooms, onion, and vermouth. Cook gently over medium heat until the vegetables are tender and the liquid is all but evaporated, about 5 minutes. Turn the mixture into a 9 x 13-inch baking dish.

Pour the prepared Popover Crust over the turkey mixture, or if you are following the alternate pastry recipe, combine the eggs and milk together in a medium-size bowl until well blended, then gradually beat in the flour until the batter is smooth. Add the butter and mix well. Pour the batter over the turkey mixture.

Bake for 15 minutes, then reduce oven temperature to 350°F and continue baking for approximately 15 more minutes, or until the pudding is puffed and golden. Serve immediately.

~ Chicken and Chile Pie ~

Basically a crustless quiche, this pie is a marvelous choice for diet watchers—low in fat and calories, yet rich in flavor.
Serves 6 to 8

8 canned green chiles, drained, seeded, and cut into strips
2 whole boneless, skinless chicken breasts (about 3/4 pound)
1 tablespoon extra virgin olive oil
4 ounces tofu
1/4 cup plain yogurt
2 large eggs
2 large egg whites
Generous dash Tabasco or other hot pepper sauce or to taste
1 teaspoon ground cumin
10 ounces Monterey Jack or other low-fat cheese, grated
Paprika and chopped fresh parsley for garnish

Preheat the oven to 400°F.

Lightly oil a 10-inch pie pan. Lay the green chile strips over the bottom and sides of the pan and set aside. Cut the chicken into 1-inch chunks. Heat the oil in a medium-size skillet and sauté the chicken pieces until they are cooked through, approximately 8 to 10 minutes.

Combine the tofu, yogurt, eggs, and egg whites with the Tabasco and cumin in the workbowl of a food processor or blender. Puree until smooth.

Layer the cheese and diced chicken in the chile-lined pan and pour the tofu mixture over all. Sprinkle liberally with paprika and parsley for color. Bake 1 hour, or until a knife inserted in the center of the pie comes out clean. Allow the pie to set for 10 minutes before cutting into wedges to serve.

~ Tortilla Stack ~

THE CUISINE of Mexico combines native and Spanish elements, both clearly apparent here. In this main-dish pie, flour or corn tortillas take the place of a pastry crust, making for a versatile and satisfying meal. Vegetarians can try the bean variation given in the recipe.
Serves 6

1/4 cup extra virgin olive oil or vegetable broth
1 bunch scallions, including green tops, diced
2 cups diced cooked chicken or one 16-ounce can black-eyed peas, black
    beans, or pink beans, undrained
1/2 cup salsa, mild to hot, depending on taste
1 cup pitted black olives, chopped
2 cups shredded Monterey Jack cheese
2 cups light sour cream
1 package corn or flour tortillas (one dozen)

Preheat the oven to 350°F.

Heat the oil or broth in a skillet or sauté pan over high heat. Add the scallions and sauté just until wilted. Add the chicken or beans and salsa and blend. Remove from the heat. In a separate bowl, combine the olives, cheese, and sour cream. Lightly grease the bottom of a pie plate or microwave-safe baking dish. Place one tortilla in the center of the pie plate and top with a layer of the chicken and salsa mixture. Place another tortilla over the chicken and spread it with a layer of the cheese and olive mixture. Repeat the layering until the pie is complete, ending with a layer of the cheese and olive mixture.

Bake in the preheated oven for 40 to 45 minutes, or until the cheese is melted and bubbly. Remove from oven and allow the pie to stand for a few minutes before cutting into wedges.

To bake in the microwave, cover the baking dish loosely and microwave for 15 to 20 minutes on high. Since most microwave ovens do not brown, sprinkle the top with paprika, vegetable seasoning, or chopped fresh cilantro for added color before serving.

Tex-Mex Polenta Pie

DEFINITELY a dish of mixed pedigree, this is easy, economical, and wonderfully satisfying.

Serves 6 to 8

1 recipe Polenta (page 15)
1 pound mild cheddar cheese, cubed
1/2 cup black olives, Calamata or Greek-style, pitted and chopped
3 cloves garlic, minced
1 medium-size onion, chopped
One 3-ounce jar pimentos, drained and chopped
1 bunch scallions, including green tops, chopped
1/2 cup chopped canned green chiles or 1/2 cup chopped red bell pepper
    and two chopped pickled jalapeño peppers
1 cup plain tomato sauce, canned or homemade
1 tablespoon ground cumin
1 tablespoon oregano

Preheat the oven to 425°F.

Prepare the polenta as directed and bake for 15 minutes.

Mix the remaining ingredients together in a large bowl and spread over the hot crust. Return the pan to the oven and continue baking for 15 to 20 minutes, or until the cheese is melted and bubbly.

~ Shaker Fish Pie ~

LIKE THE famed Shaker furniture designs, this recipe is practical, simple, and elegant.

Serves 6

1 recipe No-roll Pie Pastry (page 24)
1 medium-size onion, chopped
2 stalks celery including leaves, diced
3 tablespoons butter or extra virgin olive oil
1 pound mild-flavored fish fillets, such as flounder, sole, or porgy
2 tablespoons snipped fresh parsley
1 teaspoon marjoram
1/2 teaspoon nutmeg
1 teaspoon salt
Freshly ground pepper to taste
2 tablespoons all-purpose flour
1 cup light cream or evaporated low-fat milk
1/3 cup bread crumbs

Preheat the oven to 425°F.

Line a 10-inch pie plate with the pastry, crimp the edges as desired, and bake for 15 minutes. Remove from the oven and reduce heat to 325°F.

Sauté the onions and celery in the butter over high heat. When the onions are translucent, add the fish fillets and continue cooking until the fish can be broken into chunks with a fork. Add the seasonings and flour and blend, cooking for an additional 2 minutes. Reduce the heat to low. Add the cream all at once and simmer, stirring constantly, until the mixture is thickened and bubbly, approximately 3 minutes. Turn the mixture into the prepared crust, top with the bread crumbs, and bake for 35 minutes.

Alsatian Fish and Potato Pie

V ERY FRENCH and very, very good! For an extra touch, use a Rye Crust (page 12) with a pinch or two of caraway seed added.

Serves 6 to 8

1/2 recipe Basic Pie Crust (page 13)
2 slices bacon, cut into 1/2-inch pieces
1 large onion, chopped
1/4 cup evaporated low-fat milk
1 large egg
1/4 cup sour cream
Cracked fresh pepper to taste
1/4 teaspoon nutmeg
1 pound new potatoes, boiled and cut into 1/4-inch slices
1 pound firm-fleshed mild-flavored fish fillets, such as haddock, cod, scrod,
*   etc., cut into 1-inch chunks*
Butter or margarine (optional)

Preheat the oven to 425°F.

Line a deep-dish 9-inch pie plate with the pastry and place it in the freezer while preparing the filling.

In a medium-size skillet, fry the bacon pieces until they are crisp. Add the chopped onion and sauté until golden brown. Remove the pan from the heat. Combine the milk, egg, and sour cream with the pepper and nutmeg in a bowl.

Remove the pastry from the freezer. Assemble the pie by lining the pan with a layer of potatoes, followed by a layer of fish, followed by a layer of onions. Repeat the layering until all the ingredients are used up. Pour the milk and egg mixture over all. Dot with butter, if desired.

Place the pie in the oven and immediately reduce the oven temperature to 350°F (this allows the crust to become crispy as the temperature drops) and bake for 40 minutes, or until the filling is bubbly and lightly browned.

California
~ Crabmeat Pie ~

SAVORY crabmeat is piled in a light, crispy shell. Perfect for a summer supper.

Serves 6

1 recipe Gougère (page 16) or Confetti Crust (page 23)

10 ounces lump crabmeat or crabmeat substitute

3 scallions, including green tops, chopped

1/4 cup pitted, chopped black olives

1 ripe avocado, peeled, pitted, and mashed

1/2 cup sour cream

1/2 cup mayonnaise

Juice of one lemon

Salt, freshly cracked pepper, and Tabasco or other hot
     pepper sauce to taste

1 cup grated cheddar cheese

Additional olives for garnish

Preheat the oven to 425°F.

For the gougère, bake for 10 minutes, then reduce the temperature to 375°F and continue baking until the crust is puffed and golden brown, 15 to 20 minutes. Remove from the oven and cool. (Note: Unfilled gougère puffs considerably during baking, but will lose volume when removed from the oven to allow for filling.) For the Confetti Crust, bake at 375°F for 15 minutes and cool.

Combine the crabmeat, scallions, olives, avocado, sour cream, mayonnaise, and lemon juice. Add the seasonings to taste. Spread the filling over the cooled crust. Top with grated cheese and garnish with olives. Chill thoroughly before serving.

~❧ Shrimp Boat ❧~

Fresh herbs and shrimp combine for a new definition of the light fantastic. Use either of the pastry suggestions given below, or use a baked plain pizza crust (page 96) for equally wonderful results.
6 to 8 servings

1 recipe No-roll Pie Pastry (page 24) or Olive Oil Crust (page 11)
2 tablespoons butter or margarine
1 tablespoon extra virgin olive oil
2 scallions, including green tops, minced
2 large cloves garlic, minced
1/4 cup chopped fresh basil leaves
1/4 cup chopped fresh parsley
2 tablespoons chopped fresh oregano leaves or 3/4 teaspoon dried
2 teaspoons chopped fresh rosemary leaves or 3/4 teaspoon dried
1/4 cup dry white wine
12 large tiger shrimp, cleaned, shelled, and deveined
4 ounces whole-milk or part-skim ricotta cheese
Juice of 1 lemon
1/4 cup canned artichoke hearts, drained and diced

Preheat the oven to 425°F.

Line a 10-inch tart pan with a removable bottom with your choice of pastry. Bake for 15 to 18 minutes, or until the crust is a very light golden. Remove from the oven.

Heat the butter and olive oil in a medium-size sauté pan. Add the scallions, garlic, herbs, and wine and cook, stirring constantly, until the herbs are wilted. Add the shrimp and cook just until they are pink and the liquid is all but evaporated, 3 to 4 minutes. Remove from the heat and set aside.

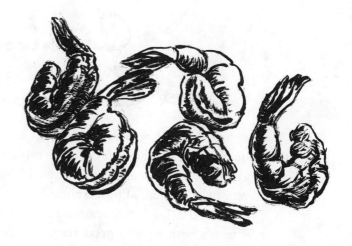

Combine the ricotta cheese and lemon juice and spread in a layer over the prepared crust. Top with a thin layer of the herb and onion mixture, followed by a layer of the artichokes. Arrange the shrimps in a pinwheel design over all and top with any remaining herb and onion mixture. Bake just until the filling is bubbly and lightly browned, 10 to 12 minutes.

Charleston
❧ Shrimp Pie ❦

IN MANY old recipes, such as this one, which dates from colonial times, a traditional pastry crust is replaced with simple and economical ingredients, in this case, leftover bread. The bread and eggs combine to form a light, puffed, almost soufflé-like result. The lighter the bread, the lighter the pie, but I have experimented with whole grain and even light rye breads with equally good results. When making this pie, use whole milk or, for a creamier texture and less fat, evaporated low-fat milk as plain skim milk doesn't bind the filling properly.

Serves 6

5 slices any type bread, cubed

1 cup whole milk or evaporated low-fat milk

2 large eggs, beaten

1 pound small or medium-size shrimp, cleaned, peeled, and deveined,
    uncooked

2 tablespoons extra virgin olive or grapeseed oil

1 bunch scallions, including green tops, chopped

1/2 cup chopped green or red bell pepper

1 tablespoon chopped fresh parsley

1 teaspoon salt or lemon pepper seasoning

1 1/2 tablespoons Worcestershire sauce

Generous dash Tabasco or other hot pepper sauce to taste

2 to 3 tablespoons dry sherry

Preheat the oven to 375°F.

In a large bowl, soak the bread cubes in the milk combined with the eggs for 10 minutes. Combine with the remaining ingredients, taking care that the shrimp and vegetables are evenly distributed throughout.

Lightly grease the bottom and sides of a 2 1/2-quart casserole. Turn the shrimp mixture into the dish and bake for 40 to 45 minutes, or until puffed and lightly browned.

Oyster Pie

THIS RECIPE is for those lucky enough to live in an area where the cost of a quart of fresh oysters isn't prohibitive—and for the rest of us, too, because no matter what the cost, there are always times when something this good is just too good to pass up.

Serves 6 to 8

1 recipe Confetti Crust (page 23) for the bottom crust
1 sheet packaged frozen or homemade Puff Pastry (pages 20-21) for the
*   top crust*
4 tablespoons butter or margarine
2 tablespoons all-purpose flour
1/2 teaspoon salt
Freshly ground pepper to taste
1/2 teaspoon poultry seasoning
3/4 cup light cream or evaporated low-fat milk
1/4 cup dry sherry
Generous dash Worcestershire sauce
1 quart large, fresh, shucked oysters, drained
4 large eggs, hard-boiled, peeled, and sliced

Preheat the oven to 400°F.

Prebake the bottom crust for 10 minutes. In a medium-size saucepan, heat the butter over medium heat until it foams. Add the flour, salt, pepper, and poultry seasoning to make a roux. Cook for 2 minutes, stirring constantly. Add the cream and sherry all at once, and continue cooking until thickened and smooth, about 3 minutes. Remove from the heat, add the Worcestershire sauce, and blend. Layer the oysters and the egg slices in the prepared crust. Pour the milk mixture over all. Top with a circle of puff

pastry, or another pastry of your choice. Bake for 15 minutes, then reduce the oven temperature to 350°F and continue baking for an additional 30 minutes, or until the crust is golden brown.

Variation:

Chicken and Oyster Pie: A somewhat more economical version of this pie can be made by substituting 2 cups diced cooked chicken for half the oysters. Sauté 2 tablespoons grated onion and 1 stalk chopped celery in the butter. Make the roux and proceed as above.

Deep-dish Down East Clam Pie

THOUGH fresh is still best, the wide availability of canned clams makes this a pie even the landlocked among us can enjoy.

Serves 6 to 8

1 recipe No-roll Pie Pastry (page 24) or Sourdough Pie Crust (pages 18-19)

4 slices bacon, cooked until crisp, drained on paper towels, and crumbled

3 cups ground fresh clams, with their liquor, or three 8-ounce cans chopped clams, with their liquid

3/4 cup regular or low-fat milk

1/2 teaspoon marjoram

1/2 teaspoon thyme

1/2 teaspoon salt

Freshly ground pepper to taste

1 cup crushed oyster crackers

Generous dash Worcestershire sauce

Generous dash Tabasco or other hot pepper sauce or to taste

4 tablespoons butter

Preheat the oven to 425°F.

On a lightly floured surface, roll out the dough large enough to cover a 9 x 9-inch baking dish or a 1 1/2-quart casserole.

In a large bowl, combine the bacon, clams and their liquor, milk, seasonings, and cracker crumbs. Season to taste with Worcestershire and Tabasco sauce. Generously butter the baking dish and turn the clam mixture into it. Dot with additional butter, if desired. Top with the pastry, sealing the edge of the pastry over the edge of the pan. Cut 3 or 4 deep slashes in the pastry to allow steam to escape during baking. Bake for 15 minutes, then reduce the oven temperature to 350°F and continue baking for an additional 20 minutes, or until the crust is golden brown and the filling is bubbly.

Wild Mushroom
~ Torte ~

THIS TORTE is a subtle and earthy combination of potatoes and wild mushrooms. Though many European varieties of mushrooms are currently available fresh or dried at specialty and food shops all over the country, they can still be relatively expensive. Therefore, I suggest combining a small portion of these specialty mushrooms with a portion of commercially grown fresh mushrooms, for all of the flavor at a fraction of the cost.

Serves 6 to 8

1 recipe Puff Pastry (pages 20-21) or one 16-ounce package frozen puff pastry or 1 recipe Sourdough Pie Crust (pages 18-19)
4 tablespoons (1/2 stick) unsalted butter
2 pounds yellow onions, sliced paper-thin
1 pound fresh white cultivated mushrooms, cleaned
4 ounces fresh chanterelle, porcini, cremini, oyster, or morel mushrooms, sliced
2 tablespoons all-purpose flour
1/4 cup bourbon or cognac
1 cup heavy cream or evaporated milk
2 tablespoons chopped fresh parsley
Salt and freshly ground pepper to taste
5 medium-size red-skinned new potatoes, washed and thinly sliced
1 large egg, beaten (optional)

Preheat the oven to 375°F.

On a lightly floured surface, roll out half of the pastry to line the bottom and sides of an 11-inch tart or springform pan. Roll out the remaining dough in a circle large enough to cover and set aside.

In a large skillet, melt the butter over medium heat until it foams. Add the onions and fry gently. Remove the stems from the white mushrooms and reserve for another use. Add the mushroom caps and remaining mushrooms to the skillet. When all of the liquid has evaporated, stir in the flour to make a roux, and cook 1 to 2 minutes, stirring constantly. Add the bourbon, cream, parsley, salt, and pepper, simmer gently for 5 minutes, or until the mixture is thickened and smooth.

Place one third of the potato slices in concentric circles over the bottom layer of pastry, covering it completely. Cover the slices with half of the mushroom mixture. Repeat the layering process, ending with a layer of potatoes.

Gently place the top crust over all and crimp the edges together very firmly to seal. Brush with the beaten egg to glaze, if desired. Score the top of the pastry in a decorative pattern to allow steam to escape during baking. Bake for 50 minutes to 1 hour, or until the pastry is golden brown. Allow the torte to stand 15 minutes before cutting into wedges to serve.

Pesto Tart

E ASY AND satisfying—you'll never know you're eating light!

Serves 6

1 recipe Olive Oil Crust (page 11)
1/2 cup pesto, preferably homemade (see note below)
2 cups whole milk or part-skim ricotta cheese
1 large egg
1/2 teaspoon nutmeg
6 to 8 sun-dried tomatoes packed in olive oil, drained

Preheat the oven to 350°F.

On a lightly floured surface, roll out the pastry to line a 9-inch tart pan with a removable bottom.

Spread the pesto evenly over the bottom of the crust. In a medium-size bowl, combine the ricotta, egg, and nutmeg and spoon it evenly over the pesto. Arrange the sun-dried tomatoes in a decorative pattern over the top.

Bake the tart for 30 to 40 minutes, or until the crust and filling are lightly browned.

Note: To make 1/2 cup pesto, combine 1/2 cup fresh basil leaves, 1 tablespoon pine nuts, 2 cloves garlic, and 3 tablespoons extra virgin olive oil in a food processor and process until smooth.

Bacon, Onion, and Apple Tart

THIS IS a recipe influenced both by Amish and Canadian settlers. Here sweet red onions are piled in a crisp crust with bacon and sliced apples. For another variation, try this with kielbasa or a similar smoked sausage.

Serves 6 to 8

1/2 recipe Basic Pie Crust (page 13)
3 large red onions, thinly sliced
2 large crisp apples, peeled, cored, and thinly sliced
1/2 teaspoon salt
1 teaspoon freshly ground pepper
2 tablespoons all-purpose flour
1/3 cup light cream or evaporated low-fat milk
1/4 pound sliced or Canadian-style bacon

Preheat the oven to 425°F. Prebake the prepared crust for 15 minutes, remove it from the oven, and reduce the temperature to 350°F.

In a large bowl, mix the onions and apples. Season them with salt and pepper and toss with the flour to coat. Pile the onions and apples in the prebaked crust and pour the cream over all. Top with bacon strips. Bake until the bacon is crisp and the onions are tender, 60 to 70 minutes.

Note: If using Canadian-style bacon, stew the onions gently in 1/4 cup water until translucent, then mix the onions with the apples and proceed according to the recipe, adjusting the baking time to 45 minutes.

Pies

Pissaladière

Y ET ANOTHER example of just why French cuisine is famous the world over, this fantastic onion tart is traditionally made using a yeast-based crust, making it a close cousin to the Italian foccacia. A few kitchen experiments, however, have yielded this version baked in a sourdough crust for an incomparable flavor combination that is great served hot or cold.

Serves 4 to 6

1 recipe Sourdough Pie Crust (pages 18-19)
1/4 cup extra virgin olive oil
3 large cloves garlic, crushed
2 1/2 pounds Vidalia or sweet red onions, peeled and thinly sliced
1 teaspoon chopped fresh thyme or 1/2 teaspoon dried
Salt and freshly ground pepper to taste
One 2-ounce can anchovy fillets, drained
One 2-ounce can rolled anchovy fillets with capers, drained
1/2 cup oil-cured black olives, pitted and chopped

Preheat the oven to 425°F.

On a lightly floured surface, roll out the pastry in a circle large enough to line a 10-inch tart pan with a removable bottom. Line the pan, trim any excess pastry from the edges, and set aside.

In a large skillet, heat the oil over low heat, add the garlic and onions, cover, and cook very slowly, stirring occasionally, for 30 minutes. (Note: Very slow cooking enhances the sweet flavor of the onions which is essential to this recipe.) The onions should be very limp, but not browned. Add the thyme, salt, and pepper and remove from the heat and cool.

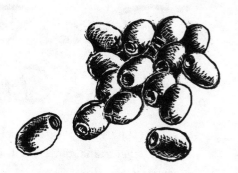

Spread the onion mixture over the prepared crust. Lay the flat anchovies out in a pinwheel design. Alternate the rolled anchovies and olives over the pie in a decorative pattern.

Bake for 10 minutes, then reduce the oven temperature to 350°F and continue baking for an additional 20 minutes.

Potato, Blue Cheese, and ~ Chive Tart ~

COMPLEMENT this selection with a light white wine and a salad. Vegetarians can omit the prosciutto, but be sure to choose a richer pastry if you do.
Serves 6

1/2 recipe Basic Pie Crust (page 13)
1/4 pound prosciutto, sliced paper-thin
1 large or 2 small red-skinned potatoes, sliced very thin
2 cups sour cream
3/4 cup crumbled blue cheese (approximately 6 ounces)
1/2 cup chopped fresh chives
1/2 cup whole or skim milk
1 tablespoon butter or margarine

Preheat the oven to 425°F.

On a lightly floured surface, roll out the pastry in a circle large enough for a 9- or 10-inch pie plate. Lay the pastry in the pan and crimp the edges as desired.

Lay slices of prosciutto in a single layer over the pastry. Follow that with a layer of potatoes, and a layer of sour cream. Sprinkle with the cheese and chives. Repeat the layering until all the ingredients are used up, ending with a layer of potatoes. Carefully pour the milk over all. Dot with butter or margarine. Bake for 1 hour, or until the potatoes are golden brown and slightly crisp.

French-Canadian
~ Toutière ~

A CLASSIC dish, this time lightened and enhanced by the wonderful addition of apples. This is an economical use of leftovers that makes for a satisfying and hearty winter supper.
Serves 6 to 8

1 recipe Old-time Pie Paste (page 9) or Whole-wheat Crust (page 12)
2 tablespoons instant mashed potato flakes (optional)
2 large Granny Smith or Macoun apples, peeled, cored, and diced
1 1/2 to 2 cups leftover cooked pork, coarsely chopped
1 medium-size onion, coarsely chopped
1 cup mashed potatoes
1 cup leftover gravy or 1 cup chicken broth and 2 tablespoons all-purpose flour
1/4 cup red wine
2 tablespoons Worcestershire sauce or to taste

Preheat the oven to 375°F.

Line a 10-inch pie plate with the pastry. Roll out the top crust and set aside. Sprinkle the bottom crust with instant mashed potato flakes if desired for added crispness.

Combine the remaining ingredients in a medium-size mixing bowl until well blended. Turn into the prepared crust and top with the remaining crust, folding top edge over bottom edge to seal. Trim as necessary. Crimp the edge with your fingertips or the tines of a fork. Prick the top crust to allow steam to escape and bake for 50 to 60 minutes, or until the crust is lightly browned. Allow the toutière to sit for 10 minutes before serving.

Pies

Leek and Sausage Pie

THIS PIE has its roots in French country cooking, although this version is considerably lightened by the use of lean varieties of sausage and the use of evaporated low-fat milk rather than the more traditional heavy cream. For an even heartier version of this wonderful main-dish pie, try adding one or two thinly sliced cooked potatoes. Serve with a light red wine and enjoy.

Serves 4 to 6

1/2 pound 80% lean kielbasa or similar smoked-style turkey sausage, sliced
    into 1/4-inch rounds
4 large leeks, washed and sliced into 1/4-inch rounds
3/4 cup water
1 large egg yolk, beaten
1/3 cup evaporated low-fat milk
1 sheet packaged frozen puff pastry, thawed, or 1/2 recipe **Puff Pastry**
    (pages 20-21)
1 large egg yolk mixed with 1 tablespoon water for glazing (optional)

Preheat the oven to 425°F.

    In a large skillet, gently fry the sausage over medium heat until lightly browned. Add the leeks and water. Stew the leeks until translucent and most of the liquid has evaporated. Cool slightly and add the egg yolk and milk. Mix until the filling binds together. Turn the mixture into a 9 x 13-inch or 1 1/2-quart baking dish or a 10-inch soufflé dish.

Roll out the puff pastry to fit the top of the baking dish. Lay the pastry over the dish and brush with the egg yolk mixed with water to glaze, if desired. Bake for 15 minutes, then reduce the oven temperature to 350°F, and continue baking until the pastry is puffed and golden, approximately 20 minutes more. Allow the pie to sit for 10 minutes before serving.

ᴥ Cranberry Pork Pie ᴥ

PORK AND fruit are a natural combination that seems to show up in many cuisines around the world. In this uniquely American selection, tangy cranberries add a special touch to tender, savory pork. Different and delightful.

Serves 6

1/4 cup all-purpose flour
1 teaspoon poultry seasoning
1 teaspoon ground sage
Freshly ground pepper to taste
2 pounds lean boneless pork, cut into 1 1/2-inch cubes
2 slices bacon, diced
1 1/4 cups whole fresh cranberries
1/2 cup firmly packed brown sugar
Grated zest of 1 orange (orange part only)
1 cup hot water
1 recipe Buttermilk Biscuit Crust (page 17)

Preheat the oven to 400°F.

Combine the flour, poultry seasoning, sage, and pepper in a plastic bag. Add the pork cubes and dredge in the flour mixture to coat them thoroughly.

In a large skillet, combine the bacon pieces and pork cubes. Stir-fry over high heat until they are well browned on all sides. Drain off any fat. Place the meat in a 1 1/2-quart casserole.

Toss the cranberries with the sugar and orange zest and distribute them evenly over the meat. Pour the water over all. Cover and bake for 25 minutes.

Meanwhile, prepare the biscuit crust. Drop by tablespoonfuls over the pork mixture. Return to the oven and continue baking, uncovered, an additional 20 minutes, or until the crust is puffed and golden brown.

Broccoli and Cauliflower Pie

I ONCE MADE this pie with purple broccoli and green cauliflower. In
the orange cheddar cheese crust, it was spectacular!

Serves 6 to 8

1 recipe Cheddar Cheese Crust (page 22)
1 cup broccoli florets, broken into small chunks
1 cup cauliflower florets, broken into small chunks
1 tablespoon butter or margarine
1 medium-size onion, chopped
2 tablespoons all-purpose flour
1 cup evaporated skim milk
1 teaspoon salt
1/2 teaspoon thyme
Freshly ground pepper
3 large eggs, slightly beaten

Preheat the oven to 400°F.

Press the prepared pastry into the bottom and sides of a 10-inch pie plate. Set aside.

In a medium-size saucepan, steam the broccoli and cauliflower together just until tender. Cool slightly and place in the prepared crust.

Using the same saucepan, if desired, melt the butter over medium heat until it foams. Add the onion and sauté just until tender. Stir in the flour to make a roux, and continue cooking for 2 minutes. Add the milk and the seasonings. Continue cooking, stirring constantly, until slightly thickened, approximately 2 minutes. Cool slightly and whisk in the eggs to blend well. Pour over the broccoli mixture.

Bake for 15 minutes, then reduce the oven temperature to 375°F and bake an additional 20 minutes, or until a knife inserted into the center of the pie comes out clean.

Harvest Vegetable Pie

EGGPLANT slices provide the "crust" for this wonderful vegetarian selection, a great dish for those days in autumn when fresh produce is abundant.

Serves 6

1 large eggplant (approximately 2 pounds), peeled and sliced
    1/4 inch thick
2 large eggs, lightly beaten
2 cups seasoned bread crumbs
4 large ripe, firm tomatoes, peeled and coarsely chopped
2 medium-size zucchini, yellow summer squash, or lita squash, sliced into
    rounds
3 cloves garlic, minced
1/2 cup fresh basil leaves
1/2 cup crumbled feta cheese
1/2 cup pine nuts (optional)
1 tablespoon extra virgin olive oil

Preheat the oven to 350°F.

Dip the eggplant slices first in egg, then in bread crumbs to coat. Line a 10-inch pie or tart pan with the eggplant slices. Bake until the slices are lightly browned, approximately 20 minutes.

Meanwhile, combine the tomatoes, squash, garlic, and basil in a nonstick saucepan. Cook over low heat until the sauce thickens, about 25 minutes.

Pour the sauce over the prepared eggplant slices. Top with the feta cheese and pine nuts, if desired, and sprinkle with olive oil. Cover the pan with aluminum foil and bake for 70 to 75 minutes.

~🙰 Indian Samosas 🙰~

SAMOSAS are a traditional fried pastry with a variety of fillings. Rich and savory, they can be made as either individual pies or in a smaller version for appetizers. Calorie watchers can make a baked version, but I've found that, because the pastry crust is very low in fat, these tend to lose something in the translation when baked. What I do recommend is frying in canola oil, one of the highest in unsaturated fat, draining thoroughly and finishing by reheating them in the oven.

Makes about 16 individual pies or 36 appetizers

1 recipe Yogurt Pastry (page 26)
2 tablespoons vegetable oil
1 medium-size onion, minced
2 cloves garlic, minced
1/2 pound lean ground lamb
1 carrot, diced
1/2 cup peas
1 small potato, peeled and diced
1 tablespoon curry powder or more to taste
1 teaspoon salt
2 teaspoons cumin
1/2 teaspoon ground coriander
1/4 cup plain yogurt
4 cups canola oil for frying

Prepare the Yogurt Pastry as directed and chill for 2 hours.

In a medium-size sauté pan heat the oil and brown the onions, garlic, and lamb over high heat. Add the carrot, peas, and potato. Stir-fry for 10 minutes, or until the potato is tender. Add the seasonings and yogurt, reduce heat, and continue cooking 10 minutes longer. Cool the filling before assembling the pastries.

On a lightly floured surface roll out one fourth of the dough to a thickness of approximately 1/8 inch. For individual pies, cut into 4-inch circles. (For appetizers, make circles approximately 2 1/2 inches in diameter.)

Place 2 heaping tablespoons of the prepared filling on one half of each circle. (Reduce the amount accordingly for appetizers.) Fold the dough over turnover-style, and crimp the edges together to seal. Place the samosas on a baking sheet, cover with a damp towel, and refrigerate while preparing the remaining pastries.

Heat the oil in a kettle or deep-fryer to a temperature of 375°F. Fry the pastries, a few at a time, until light brown on both sides, approximately 4 minutes per side. Drain thoroughly on paper towels and keep warm in a 300°F oven while frying the remaining pastries.

Variation: For shrimp filling, omit the curry powder, substitute 1/4 cup chopped tomato for the carrot and 1/2 pound cleaned, peeled, and chopped shrimp for the lamb.

Pirozhky

THESE ARE a Russian cousin to the popular Polish pirogi. They can be baked or fried, in which case they are called paramach. Either way, these individual pies are delicious with any number of fillings. Try any of the ones given here, or experiment with your own.
Makes 18 pirozhky

1 recipe Cream Cheese Pastry (page 25) or Yogurt Pastry (page 26)

CABBAGE FILLING
2 tablespoons butter or margarine
1/2 head cabbage, finely chopped
1 large onion, finely chopped
1 teaspoon caraway seeds
2 large eggs, hard-boiled and chopped
1/2 teaspoon salt
1 teaspoon sugar

In a large sauté pan, melt the butter. Add the cabbage and the onion, cover, and cook slowly over low heat until the vegetables are translucent, about 20 minutes. Add the caraway seeds, eggs, salt, and sugar and mix well.

MEAT FILLING

2 medium-size onions, chopped
1 pound ground beef
3 tablespoons minced fresh dill or 1 teaspoon dried
1 tablespoon all-purpose flour
1 tablespoon Worcestershire sauce (optional)
3 tablespoons ketchup
Salt and freshly ground pepper to taste

In a large sauté pan, brown the onions and beef together over high heat until the beef loses its pink color. Add the dill and continue cooking until it is wilted. Add the flour, Worcestershire sauce, ketchup, salt, and pepper and mix well.

MUSHROOM FILLING

4 cups sliced mushrooms, cleaned and thinly sliced (approximately 1
    pound; mix a portion of wild mushrooms such as cremini, portobello,
    oyster, or even shiitake mushrooms with a portion of fresh mushrooms
    for added flavor)
4 tablespoons butter or extra virgin olive oil
2 medium-size onions, chopped
3 tablespoons sour cream or light sour cream
Salt and freshly ground pepper to taste

Over high heat, lightly sauté the mushrooms in two tablespoons of the butter until tender. Set aside. In the remaining two tablespoons of butter sauté the onions until golden. Just before filling the pirozhky, combine the onions and mushrooms with the remaining ingredients.

TO ASSEMBLE THE PIROZHKY

Preheat the oven to 400°F.

Pies

Roll out the pastry on a lightly floured surface and cut it into eighteen 4-inch circles. Place 2 heaping tablespoons of filling on one half of each circle. Fold the other half over and crimp the edges to seal. Place the pirozhky on a baking sheet, covering them with a damp towel while preparing the remaining pastries. Prick each pirozhky with a fork to allow steam to escape. Bake for 20 minutes, or until golden brown.

For Paramach: Prepare Pirozhky using Yogurt Pastry and the meat filling. Heat 4 cups of vegetable or canola oil in a deep, heavy skillet or deep-fryer to a temperature of 375°F. Fry the pastries, a few at a time, for approximately 4 minutes on each side, or until they are golden. Drain on paper towels.

⊸ Kulebiaka ⊱

ANOTHER Russian specialty, this loaf-shaped pie is the ideal buffet dish, particularly since it is delicious reheated and will improve in flavor if made ahead of time. Various pastries can be used in making this dish. Any pastry used for baked pirozhky is excellent, as is puff pastry which gives an added elegant touch.
Serves 10 to 12

1 recipe Basic Pie Crust (page 13)
1 large egg yolk, beaten

BEEF FILLING
6 tablespoons butter or margarine
3 medium-size onions, chopped
4 cloves garlic, minced
2 pounds ground sirloin or 1 pound ground sirloin and 1 pound ground veal
1/4 cup beef stock
2 teaspoons salt or to taste
1/2 teaspoon freshly ground pepper
4 large eggs, hard-boiled
1/2 teaspoon thyme
1/4 cup minced fresh dill or 3 teaspoons dried
1/4 cup minced fresh parsley

In a large skillet, melt the butter and add the onions, garlic, and meat. Cook until the onions are translucent and the meat loses all its pink color. Add the beef stock and salt and pepper to taste. Cool.

Preheat the oven to 350°F.

Divide the pastry into two equal portions. On a lightly floured surface, roll the first portion into a rectangle large enough to line the bottom and sides of a large loaf pan, approximately 10 x 6 x 2 1/2 inches. The dough should overlap the sides of the pan by 1/2 inch all around. Roll out the second portion into a rectangle approximately 12 x 6 1/2 inches, or large enough to form the top of the "loaf."

Slice the eggs and place a layer of egg slices on the bottom of the pastry-lined loaf pan. Sprinkle with the thyme, dill, and parsley. Top with a generous layer of meat. Repeat the layering, ending with a layer of the meat mixture and mounding the top into a loaf shape. Compress lightly, being careful not to tear the pastry.

Place the top layer of pastry over all. With wet fingertips, pinch together the top and bottom layers of pastry very firmly to seal. Cut three slashes in the pastry to allow steam to escape. Brush the pastry with beaten egg yolk to glaze, if desired. Bake 40 to 45 minutes, or until lightly browned. To serve, cut into slices as you would a loaf of bread. Kulebiaka may be served warm or cold.

SALMON FILLING

Two 16-ounce cans salmon, drained and boned
2 tablespoons tomato paste
Cracked fresh pepper to taste
1/2 teaspoon Tabasco or other hot pepper sauce
1 tablespoon curry powder
Juice of 1 lemon
2 tablespoons canola or other oil
6 shallots, chopped
1/4 cup minced fresh dill or 3 teaspoons dried
4 ounces chopped fresh wild mushrooms (optional)
2 large eggs, hard-boiled and chopped
2 cups cooked rice
3 to 4 tablespoons butter or margarine

Place the salmon in a large bowl. Season it to taste with the tomato paste, pepper, Tabasco, curry powder, and lemon juice, breaking up the salmon as you combine the ingredients. Set aside.

In a medium-size pan heat the oil and sauté the shallots, dill, and mushrooms. Cool slightly and combine with the chopped eggs.

Line the loaf pan with half the pastry as described above. Spread about two thirds of the cooked rice in a layer over the pastry, keeping to within 1/2 inch of the edge. Follow this with a layer of the shallot and egg mixture and dot with butter. Add a layer of the salmon mixture and repeat the layers. Proceed as above for the rest of the recipe.

~❧ Quiche ☙~

QUICHE is truly a classic among main-dish pies, and lends itself to a huge variety of tasty and satisfying variations. Although there is virtually no substitute for the egg-based custard that forms the basis for these wonderful pies, it is possible to cut fat and cholesterol by using evaporated low-fat milk in the filling instead of the traditional heavy cream, and further cutting fat and calories by using a low-fat cheese. I have given a good, all-around quiche with a number of suggested variations, but don't be shy about experimenting. It's a great way to clean out the refrigerator!

Serves 6 to 8

1/2 recipe Basic Pie Crust (page 13)
3 large eggs
1/4 teaspoon ground nutmeg
1/2 teaspoon salt
1/2 teaspoon freshly ground pepper
One 13-ounce can evaporated low-fat milk
2 cups cheese, meat, and/or vegetables (see variations below)

Preheat the oven to 425°F. Prebake the crust for 15 minutes.

Remove the crust from the oven and reduce the temperature to 375°F.

In a large bowl, whisk together the eggs, seasonings, and milk. Fill the crust with your choice of prepared vegetables, meats, and/or cheeses. Pour the custard mixture over all. Place the filled pan on a baking sheet. Bake for 40 minutes, or just until the custard is set. Allow the quiche to stand for 10 to 15 minutes before serving.

Variations:

Chèvre and Walnut Quiche

Combine 4 ounces Bucheron or Montrachet chèvre (goat cheese) and 4 ounces cream cheese. Add 3 tablespoons chopped fresh chives and 1/2 cup coarsely chopped walnuts. Fill the prebaked crust with the cheese mixture and proceed as above.

Mushroom, Leek, and Potato Quiche

In a medium-size sauté pan, heat 2 tablespoons butter over high heat until it foams. Gently sauté 1/4 pound chopped portobello, cremini, or other fresh mushrooms together with 3/4 cup chopped fresh leeks and 1 medium-size new red potato, sliced paper-thin, until the vegetables are tender. Place the mixture in the prebaked crust and top with 1/2 cup grated Swiss cheese. Proceed as above.

Ham and Cheddar Quiche

Finely chop 3 scallions, including green tops. Add 1/2 cup diced cooked ham and 1 cup grated cheddar cheese. Fill the prebaked crust with the ham mixture and proceed as above.

Sausage and Pepper Quiche

Over high heat fry 1/2 pound bulk pork or turkey sausage until browned. Add 1/2 cup chopped green or red bell pepper, 1 small onion, chopped, and 1/2 teaspoon sage. Continue cooking until the pepper is tender. Fill the prebaked crust with the mixture and proceed as above.

⊰ Pasta Frittata ⊱

The Italian frittata is somewhere between an omelette and crustless quiche. A fast and flexible recipe choice for a main-dish meal, it can incorporate any number of ingredients. This particular version uses cooked pasta to stretch the ingredients and add texture and flavor.
Serves 6

2 tablespoons extra virgin olive oil
2 cups mixed assorted vegetables, cheeses, and/or meats (see list below)
4 ounces any small pasta (tiny stars, broken thin spaghetti, small bow ties, etc.), cooked and drained
6 large eggs
1/2 cup milk
1/4 cup grated Parmesan cheese

Preheat the oven to 400°F.

Heat the oil in a large skillet over high heat, add the vegetables and sauté until tender. Add any meat and the cooked pasta and stir-fry 2 to 3 minutes. Beat the eggs and milk together and add to the skillet, along with any cheese (but not the Parmesan). Reduce the heat and continue cooking until the eggs have just begun to solidify, but are still runny. Turn the mixture into a greased 10-inch pie plate.

Bake 10 to 15 minutes, or until a knife inserted into the center of the pie comes out clean. Remove from the oven and raise the oven temperature to broil. Sprinkle with the Parmesan cheese and set under the broiler until the cheese is lightly browned and forms a crust, about 4 minutes.

Suggestions for Frittata:
    Bacon, cheddar, and onion (breakfast)

Chicken, olives, onion, and Monterey Jack
Mushrooms, onion, spinach, and Gorgonzola (vegetarian)
Sun-dried tomatoes, prosciutto (or ham), and mozzarella
Salami, provolone, and roasted bell peppers
Green pepper, onion, garlic, pepperoni, and Parmesan
Or you can create your own combinations of vegetables, meats, and cheeses.

Vegetables:

olives, sun-dried tomatoes, roasted green or red bell peppers, mushrooms, onions, scallions, garlic, or spinach

Meats:

pepperoni, salami, ham or prosciutto, smoked turkey or chicken, or cooked crumbled bacon

Cheeses:

provolone, mozzarella, Gorgonzola, cheddar, Monterey Jack, or Parmesan

⁓ Ripe Tomato Pie ⁓

T HIS IS perfect for a light summer supper, when fresh ripe tomatoes
are in abundance. For a special treat, make it with a Cheddar Cheese
Crust (page 22).
Serves 6

1/2 recipe Basic Pie Crust (page 13)
4 large ripe beefsteak-type tomatoes, peeled and sliced (about 3 pounds)
4 scallions, including green tops, finely chopped
1/4 cup chopped fresh basil or 2 generous tablespoons dried
Salt and freshly ground pepper to taste
2 1/2 teaspoons sugar
1 cup grated cheddar cheese
1/4 cup mayonnaise

Preheat the oven to 425°F.

On a lightly floured surface, roll out the pastry to a thickness of 1/8
inch. Gently lift the pastry into a 9- or 10-inch pie plate. Crimp the edges
as desired. Prick the crust all over with the tines of a fork and bake for 15
to 20 minutes, or until the crust is a light golden brown. Reduce the oven
temperature to 350°F.

Layer the tomatoes in the pie crust. Sprinkle them with the scallions
and chopped basil, then with the salt, pepper, and sugar. Mix the cheese
and mayonnaise together and spread evenly over all. Bake for 20 minutes,
or until the cheese is melted and bubbly.

Tomato, Cheese, and Basil Tart

Light and attractive, this dish is always my first choice for a late-summer supper. It is chock-full of fresh, vine-ripened tomatoes, redolent with basil, and housed in a perfect pastry—all of which rank as some of my favorite things. A warm wedge of this tart, a glass of wine, and a spectacular sunset is all that's really required to complete a great evening.
Serves 4 to 6

1 recipe Olive Oil Crust (page 11)
8 ounces St. André or other good melting cheese, well-chilled
3 large ripe tomatoes, sliced 1/4 inch thick
Extra virgin olive oil
1/2 cup fresh basil leaves, torn
3 tablespoons chopped walnuts

Preheat the oven to 425°F.

On a lightly floured surface, roll out the dough to a thickness of 1/8 inch. Place in a 9-inch tart or pie pan and crimp the edge as desired. Prick crust all over with the tines of a fork and bake until lightly browned, about 15 minutes. Remove from the oven and raise the oven temperature to broil.

Remove the rind from the cheese if necessary and cut it in thin slices, approximately 1/8 inch thick. Arrange cheese and tomato slices alternately in the crust in a single layer. Brush the tomatoes and cheese with a thin layer of olive oil. Sprinkle the basil and walnuts over the tart. Run the tart under the broiler until the cheese is completely melted, 3 to 5 minutes, and serve warm, cut in wedges.

~❧ Spanakopita ❧~

THIS CLASSIC Greek spinach pie is rich in nutrition and relatively low in fat. To further reduce fat and cholesterol in this recipe, try brushing the phyllo leaves with olive or grapeseed oil, then sprinkle with butter-flavored granules for added flavor.

Serves 6

2 tablespoons extra virgin olive oil

2 medium-size onions, chopped

2 cloves garlic, chopped

2 pounds spinach, washed, stalks removed, and chopped

2 large eggs

Pinch nutmeg

6 ounces feta cheese, crumbled

Salt and freshly ground pepper to taste

One 16-ounce package phyllo

1/4 cup melted butter or 1/4 cup oil and 2 tablespoons
   butter-flavored granules

Preheat the oven to 375°F.

Heat the oil in a pan over medium heat, add the onions and garlic, and fry until translucent. Add the spinach and cook, stirring until wilted and some of the liquid has evaporated.

Beat the eggs with nutmeg and add the cheese. Combine with the spinach mixture and season to taste with salt and pepper. Lightly oil an 11 x 17-inch baking dish. Line it with a sheet of phyllo and brush with butter. Repeat until you have five or six layers of pastry in the dish. Keep the unused sheets between damp paper towels to keep them moist while you work.

Spoon the spinach mixture over the pastry, smoothing it to the edges. Cover with the remaining phyllo sheets, brushing each with butter. Tuck or trim any edges and brush with the remaining butter or oil. Bake for 35 to 40 minutes, or until crisp and golden. Serve hot or cold.

Pizza Rustica

A DEEP-DISH country-style pizza with layers of cheese, vegetables, and country ham baked in a pastry, rather than a pizza-type crust. Delicious and especially easy!

Serves 4 to 6

1/2 recipe Basic Pie Crust (page 13) or 1 recipe Cheddar Cheese Crust
(page 22)
1 package frozen chopped spinach, thawed
2 cups whole-milk or part-skim ricotta cheese
1 large egg, beaten
1/4 pound prosciutto, lean pancetta, or country-style ham, very thinly
sliced
2 fresh tomatoes, sliced 1/4 inch thick, or 4 ounces sun-dried tomatoes in
oil, drained and chopped
1/2 cup fresh basil leaves (optional)
1/4 cup grated Parmesan cheese (optional)

Preheat the oven to 425°F.

On a lightly floured surface, roll out the dough to a thickness of approximately 1/8 inch. Lay it gently in a 9- or 10-inch pie plate and crimp the edges as desired. Prick the crust lightly all over with the tines of a fork and prebake for 10 minutes. Remove it from the oven and reduce temperature to 400°F.

Squeeze out any excess water from the spinach. Combine the ricotta and the egg and blend well. Lay the prosciutto, pancetta, or ham over the bottom and sides of the pastry. Place a layer of tomatoes over it, followed by a layer of spinach and basil. Spread half the ricotta over all. Repeat the layers, ending with a layer of ricotta. Top with Parmesan cheese, if desired. Bake 40 minutes, or until lightly browned and bubbly. Allow the pie to sit for 10 minutes before cutting into wedges to serve.

Pizza

P IZZA IS by far and away the most famous of the humble pies, and arguments rage over just what constitutes the perfect pizza. For me, the secret really lies in a good pizza crust and a selection of imaginative toppings. The following recipe will make a medium-thick crust. For a thinner crust, dispense with the initial rising, and for a thicker one, allow the crust to rise an additional 15 minutes before topping and baking.

The kneading method described is my own invention. It saves on kitchen mess and dishwashing!

Makes two 12-inch pizza crusts

FOR THE CRUST
2 cups warm (105°F) water
1 envelope dry yeast
1 teaspoon sugar
2 teaspoons salt
4 tablespoons extra virgin olive oil
5 to 6 cups all-purpose flour

*The
Humble
Pie*

In a medium-size bowl, combine the water, yeast, sugar, and salt. Allow the mixture to proof until bubbling and foamy, about 10 minutes. Mix in the oil. Add 5 cups of the flour all at once and mix thoroughly. Incorporate more flour as needed to make a stiff dough.

Lightly oil the inside of a sturdy plastic bag with at least a 1-gallon capacity. Place the dough inside the bag and close with a secure twist tie or rubber band. Knead the dough inside the bag for 10 minutes, or until it is smooth and elastic. Place the dough, bag and all, in a warm place and allow to rise for 45 minutes.

Divide the dough into two portions for two medium-size pizzas. Lightly oil your fingers and shape into 12-inch rounds, leaving a rim. Sprinkle a baking sheet with cornmeal and transfer dough rounds to the baking sheet. Preheat the oven to 500°F and transfer the bottom rack to the lowest position. Top as desired and bake until the crust is golden, about 20 minutes.

Pizza Toppings

Eggplant and Garlic Pizza
Makes one 12-inch pizza

1/4 cup extra virgin olive oil
1 small eggplant, peeled and sliced into 1/4-inch rounds
1 whole head of garlic, unpeeled
1/2 cup tomato sauce, canned or homemade
1 tablespoon fresh oregano leaves or 1/4 teaspoon dried
Grated Parmesan cheese

In a medium-size skillet, heat the oil over high heat. Fry the eggplant slices just until tender, adding more oil as necessary. Break the head of garlic into cloves, leaving the peels on, but removing any excess paper.

After the eggplant has cooked, reduce the heat and fry the garlic cloves in their skins by covering the pan and shaking it a few times during cooking, approximately 5 to 6 minutes, or until the garlic is tender. Cool.

Pop the garlic cloves from their skins. Spread tomato sauce evenly over the prepared pizza crust. Lay the eggplant slices over the sauce and distribute garlic cloves evenly over the top. Sprinkle with fresh oregano and top with a generous layer of Parmesan. Bake as instructed on page 97.

Smoked Salmon and Goat Cheese Pizza
Makes one 12-inch pizza

1/4 cup grated Parmesan cheese
4 ounces goat cheese flavored with garlic and herbs, crumbled
3 ounces smoked salmon or lox, cut into 1/2-inch strips
1/2 Vidalia or sweet red onion, thinly sliced and separated into rings
3 tablespoons chopped fresh dill or 2 teaspoons dried
Extra virgin olive oil

Spread half the Parmesan cheese over the prepared pizza crust. Distribute the crumbled goat cheese evenly over the top. Lay the salmon strips and onion rings over the cheese in a decorative pattern. Bake for 15 minutes. Remove from the oven and sprinkle with the dill and the remaining Parmesan cheese. Lightly drizzle with olive oil, return to the oven, and bake an additional 5 minutes.

Artichoke and Anchovy Pizza
Makes one 12-inch pizza

3/4 cup ricotta cheese
One 6-ounce jar marinated artichoke hearts, drained and halved
One 2-ounce can rolled anchovy fillets with capers, drained
1/2 cup oil-cured black olives, pitted and chopped
1/4 cup grated Parmesan cheese

Spread the ricotta evenly over the prepared pizza crust. Top with the artichoke hearts and anchovies. Sprinkle with chopped black olives and Parmesan cheese. Bake as instructed on page 97.

Roasted Pepper and Smoked Mozzarella Pizza with Pepperoni
Makes one 12-inch pizza

1/2 cup tomato sauce, canned or homemade
One 7-ounce jar roasted peppers, drained and cut into strips
4 ounces pepperoni, sliced into rounds
2 cups grated smoked mozzarella cheese (about 1/2 pound)
1/2 cup pitted green olives, preferably Sicilian style, chopped

Spread the tomato sauce evenly over the prepared pizza crust. Lay the strips of roasted pepper evenly over the top. Arrange the pepperoni slices over all and top with the smoked mozzarella. Sprinkle olives over all and bake as directed on page 97.

Four Cheese Pizza with Sun-dried Tomatoes
Makes one 12-inch pizza

3/4 cup ricotta cheese
1 cup grated mozzarella cheese
1/2 cup grated provolone or smoked scamorza cheese
1/4 cup grated Parmesan cheese
4 ounces sun-dried tomatoes in oil, drained

Spread the ricotta evenly over the prepared pizza crust. Top with the cheeses. Arrange sun-dried tomatoes in a decorative pattern over all. Bake as directed on page 97.

Index

Index

V

Vegetable Pie, Harvest, 76–77
Vegetables. *See specific vegetables*

W

Walnut and Chèvre Quiche, 87

Whole-wheat crust, 12
Wild Mushroom Torte, 62–63

Y

Yogurt Pastry, 26

ABOUT THE AUTHOR

Teresa Kennedy is the author of twenty-two books on a wide variety of subjects. She lives in New York with her husband and is the author of two other cookbooks, *American Pie* and *Cooking with Five Ingredients or Less*.

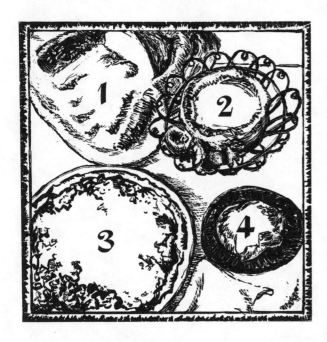